Glorious Veils
of Diane

Books by Rainie Oet

Inside Ball Lightning
Porcupine in Freefall

Glorious Veils
of Diane

by Rainie Oet

Carnegie Mellon University Press
Pittsburgh 2021

Acknowledgments

Thank you to the editors of the following journals, where some of the poems in this book originally appeared:

Bennington Review: "Blood Diary (Diane): Mesh Bags Of"
The Collagist (now known as *The Rupture*): "Blood Diary (Blood): On the Table With the Half-Eaten Carrot Cake"
Hayden's Ferry Review: "Huge Closet"
Hobart: "Hide and Seek"
jubilat: "Blood Diary (Girl Across the Street): Moth on Fire"
Mid-American Review: "Blood Diary (Blood): Come, My Beloved," "Blood Diary (Blood): Half-Moon Turning," and "Blood Diary (Diane): Hourglass of Snow"
Palette Poetry: "Blood Diary (Diane): Strawberry Red, Mirror Black" and "Blood Diary (Diane): Home"
Shenandoah: "Wanting to Erase Her Share of the Darkness"
Sycamore Review: "Blood Diary (Mother): Huge Closet"

Thank you to everyone who helped me with these poems, especially to Ariel Chu, Christopher Kennedy, Alice Blank, Bridget O'Bernstein, Bruce Smith, Ross Farrar, Joshua Burton, Ally Young, James Abele, Sarah Harwell, and Brooks Haxton.

Book design by Shruti Murali

*This book is dedicated to all the strange ghosts we were,
and to my beloved Ariel Chu.*

Contents

On January 14, 1999, Diane disappeared.

Part 1: *And the house bursts into flames*

Blood Diary (Mother):

March 14, 1993

Come into the dark kitchen to see Diane
on a step stool cooking meat.

Shhhhhhhhhhhh . . .

"Happy birthday Diane," she whispers to
me in the dark.

Blood Diary (Mother):

March 14, 2007

My daughter's hiding in the huge closet, full of shirts hanging down. I run in to try to find her, get her on my first try. The air's so thick with dresses, we can't see each other's faces. But I hug her and I run with her standing on my toes, just like old times. We're breathing hard. I say "I've got you Diane." Then I let her go.

Then it is my turn to hide as they count to ten. I'm going to play a trick on them. I'm going to disappear. I find my blind way through the clothes into a bathroom, and lock the door and breathe quietly. I wait in there for hours.

It's getting light outside. Between me and the door is a spider web. It's huge. I don't know how I got through it the first time. I only see it now because of the sun glinting off marshes in the east.

Diane is a type of sadness I have only one word for. Finally, I leave the bathroom. They've put away all the clothes. An empty hall, and my daughter's gone. I stand in it, calling out her name.

Blood Diary (Diane):

March 13, 1993

Looking off the balcony
dark wind in my face. There:
the lone, far house
under the mountains.
Am I dreaming? I think "fire."
And the house bursts into flames.

Blood Diary (Girl Across the Street):

March 15, 1994

The moth on fire in Diane's yard, across
the street, jerking to follow the trail of
its own glowing smoke, can't realize *it
is* the light it seeks, is *on fire*. The light
of this fire throws wing-shadows onto
the unbraiding smoke. Enormous, these
shadows pound against time.

I feel self-conscious, watching.

BLOOD

Diane's Dracula cape catches fire as she
dances round the bonfire holding hands
with the boy she likes, and the boy tries to
run and people are trying to tell her, but she
doesn't notice: she's grabbed his arm, pulls
him close to lift off his glittering Venetian
mask. He pushes his palm into her neck.
She spins him around and he trips into the
burning end of her long cape, and he used
hairspray so runs into the trees with his
head on fire, screaming—Diane watches
him diminishing through a photo-square
of her fingers. A kid throws a bucket of
apple water on Diane, her grandmother's
black shirt sticks to her body, she crosses
her arms over her chest. Two kids push
her back and forth, ripping at her arms.
Drenched, barefoot, she jumps through
the side of the fire with a loud hiss, escapes
through the woods.

Home, she microwaves
a soaked towel, wraps her face in it,
stumbles up the stairs to draw a bath.
Tracking mud, she knows—she can hear
her soles' sticking slap on the carpet and
tile. She undoes her grandmother's shirt,
button by button, peels everything off
except the towel on her face and sits in
the tub. Shivering, she waits for it to fill.
She hears her mother calling her name, as
if moving from room to room before each
guttural "Diane! . . ." Diane takes off the
towel and sees she's on her period, sees it

15

slipping, mixing into the muddy water. She shudders (Diane! . . . Diane! . . .) and folds herself down, over her outstretched legs, as low as she can go, so her eyes are under the water, open. She waits for the water to cover her ears. She knows how to hold her breath for a long time. It's almost there. And, there. She can't hear a thing but her heartbeat pounding the water, and the roar of the water itself, like the roar of the fire. Diane's pulled up by her hair, her mother crouching at eye level, the bathroom door off its hinges, light spilling in. "Diane," her mother says, "who are you?"

BLOOD

Ants trailing out of the hole in the mirror . . .

light cracking under their bodies . . .

down the steps . . .

BLOOD

July 9, 1993

One day Diane felt so sad watching her ceiling fan while her mother listened to an old-as-dust record of the *Goldberg Variations* in the hall. Diane felt so sad lying on the floor she wanted to scream. She wanted to scream, but she wouldn't. "Sad," she said quietly in her head. She said it out loud, "Sad. I am sad," but the voice sounded robotic, and the room felt robotic, as if all the color had been drained out of the world. Diane remembered sitting on the sand with her mother, under a white umbrella, as it started to rain—Diane's back to the sea—Diane's mother facing the sea—Diane's legs and her mother's legs touching—Diane watching her mother rub and rub and rub and rub clear lotion onto her face until it turned white. "Sad." Diane repeated it in her head a few more times. "Sad. Sad, sad, sad, sad." Diane took a nail file and slid it under her thumbnail. She pushed it deeper until it felt suddenly hot and sharp. Blood was starting to come out. Diane said the word out loud again, "Sad," but she felt more like a robot than ever. Diane tried to turn off the ceiling fan but she just made it faster so she went back on the floor and this time laid on her stomach, looking down. It was as if she was in a glass castle, looking through all the floors. Her mother stood at the very bottom, forty layers down, listening to the music, and pacing, her fingers playing with a red and blue bow in her hair.

Blood Diary (Grandmother):

November 16, 1995

Diane put her hands in the grass and took
out a piece of broken glass and looked at
me through it. "Your thumb is bleeding,"
I said. She pinched the shard harder and
I heard it going through more of her
thumb.

BLOOD

April 2, 1993

Her mother drinking milk
from cups of nails.

Breath laid whisper of fog.

Clouds above the holes in the roof.

A hot rag on the back of her mother's neck,
her mother facedown on the couch.

Still, blurred in the corner:
the deaf mop.

It's dark in the water.

        *

Diane sleeping on a red blanket
on the floor of the dark parlor.

Diane alone.

Diane breathing.

Diane's lungs filling with air, and emptying,
filling and emptying.

Diane picking the skin off her cuticles.
Diane touching,

for the first time, her blood.

Blood Diary (Diane):

I dreamed I was Mama: dreaming:

Diane is a red scaly monster with small
hands, trying to climb up my red cotton
dress: I am pushing strawberries into
Diane's mouth, pushing her forehead
down: Diane is raking me with fingernails
that I forgot to cut: red rivulets tearing
down my arms . . .

I sit up: I fell asleep with the light on,
again: shining on the always-fogged
mirror (there must be sweat behind the
glass). In the mirror: two birds of pure
darkness, thrashing around each other,
each trying to swallow the other:

Blood Diary (Diane):

May 15, 1997

A bird falls into the river.

I stop walking to pick the dead bird out of the river,

and hold it in my hands.

It isn't dead anymore, because I held it, and flies away.

Blood Diary (Diane):

There's a worm sticking out of my palm. I
keep my fist shut. It bleeds so little, slowly,
like a cut stem. I'm afraid if I rip it out
I'll die.

I sleep on dark stone, in a cave, on the
shore of a phosphorescent pond. Brown
eyes stare up from under the pond, a pale
shape of a corpse—

But there's no corpse in the water when
I splash, up to my throat, in. The ripples
slow around me, still. Water drips.

The algae regathers around me, flashing
with static. Shimmers light the stone teeth
jutting down from above the shore.

I hold my breath and curl into a ball,
floating between surface and pond floor.
My hands are open—the worm points
straight up, drops of its blood rising one
at a time.

Blood Diary (Diane):

March 13, 1993

Looking off the balcony
dark wind in my face. There:
the lone, far house
under the mountains.
Am I dreaming? I think "fire."

And nothing happens.

And it rains.
And crocuses bloom in fast-forward,
and fat vines out of the brick.

Part 2: *Come, my beloved*

BLOOD

March 15, 1995

Diane remembers a red dragon kite
whipping over the roof,
how she cut her hand
holding the string still.

*

Diane touches her eyeball
with the tip of her finger.

It's one minute after midnight,
and her birthday is over.

*

A crow slammed into the window.
It was there and gone so fast
Diane wasn't sure if it was real.

Diane's frog died
and Diane sang "Yedid Nefesh" for it
before flushing it in the toilet.
As the water spun,
she saw its legs kicking.

Blood Diary (Mother):

Today is Diane's birthday. She's holding the scissors in the moonlight, close to her hair in the mirror. She cuts and cuts, and changes. The hair grows back. Today is Diane's birthday. The floor is wet. The room is filling with pink water. Today is Diane's birthday. Where are you now? Deep underground, there is another house. It's flooded. Deep underground, there's a bottomless room, and Diane's hair is sinking through it. Diane walks to the window and looks out. She is seeing her own reflection. She is seeing a landscape filled with marshes, spreading on forever. She is seeing the sun rising.

I walk into the room. Diane disappears. I live and live. I wake up from a nightmare. In the nightmare I was mourning Diane, and then felt a shadow rising up through me, found myself shrieking, "Diane is here!" I wake up from a nightmare and repeat Diane is here, Diane is here, rubbing my throat. I climb down into a swimming pool and paddle from one side to the other. I spend some time in the center, paddling around.

BLOOD

June 6, 1999

Ants covered Diane's body until they found a wound recent enough (mosquito-scab peeled yesterday) to pile into Diane's bloodstream, where all ants dreamed of ending up one day. Though every one of these ants died by drowning in blood, they got their wish and were resolutely happy. Somewhere from many shifting points along her body all at once, Diane felt pain.

BLOOD

January 4, 1995

Diane was going to get a new sister or brother. She hoped it was a sister. She felt afraid.

Diane found a wire-hook under the bathroom sink, twisted it against her kneecap.

Diane wasn't going to get a sister after all.

"I hate you," Diane shouted down the pitch-dark and lonely hall weeks later, then whispered to herself, wet hair over her mouth, "It should have been me."

BLOOD

April 19, 1995

Diane cut her hair with safety scissors, jag-zag,
and invisible-taped it to the bald head
of her baby doll.
"You're hideous," she told it, closing its eyes.

*

Diane leaned in so close,
and opened the baby doll's eyes, so close Diane thought
the baby doll could see
the darkness of its own matte pupils
reflected in Diane's.

*

Diane closed her eyes
and saw the burned boy
taking off the burned Venetian mask
at his sink—the burned eyes.

Blood Diary (Girl Across the Street):

January 30, 1995

Diane stood at the end of her street with all her friends, throwing big chunks of ice at the 45 mph road. She loved the crush of the ice under tires, or the tires swerving to avoid. She loved especially when a school bus ran over the ice.

They jumped over the shadows of the cars passing when it was sunlight. When it wasn't, it was all shadow, and they were dead.

I watched from my window.

My parents don't allow me to ever leave the house.

Today, when they were both in the shower, I imagined going out to the end of the street, alone, and throwing chunks of ice at that busy road, too.

Blood Diary (Girl Across the Street):

March 17, 1995

Diane pretends to make a lot of noise
when her deaf grandmother touches her shoulder.

I dreamed I was a mosquito.

BLOOD

August 28, 1994

Diane couldn't coax the locust to unhinge
its hooked arms from the tree. She tried
to pry them loose, but they snapped off
in her hands and the locust fell. Diane
watched it fall to the ground, as in slow
motion, while a creepy violin soundtrack
played in her head.

BLOOD

Diane remembers her mother
crying curled into a ball
behind the couch.

Diane doesn't remember
ever feeling sad as a child.

Blood Diary (Diane):

January 1, 1999

I picked so many scabs   off my chest last night
trying to sleep   they were so small
like mites   they were my scabs
from my blood   they formed without blood

wandering my chest   I kept brushing them off
like Mama did   with me rolling
on the   memory foam
feeling my dry scabs   below me

wherever I rolled.

Blood Diary (Diane):

do you think you're alone do you
think do you think you're alone do you
think you're alone do you do you think
you're do you think you're alone alone
think you're alone do you think you're
alone do you do you think you're alone
think you're do you think you're alone
alone you're alone

not because of the air between the
firefly and its wings but because it is
irreversible

Lights on the kites at night.
They are by the waterfall.
Shadows on the clouds.

(When will I grow up?)

BLOOD

October 31, 1999

Diane stays inside this Halloween,
watching everyone through red curtains.

It isn't death she's scared of.

She hums "Lecha Dodi."

She puts a sugar cube on her tongue
whenever anyone rings the bell.

Part 3: *Hands up and open in front of her face, a blur*

BLOOD

September 15, 1996

Small fingerless hands of smoke grab
Diane when she turns her back and slam
her against the refrigerator door. They are
wrapping her eyes, throat, arms, stomach,
ankles, hands. She breathes and feels her
heartbeat in her heels on the cold tile.
They manipulate her body to open the
refrigerator door and drink milk from the
jug, sloppily. It runs down her shirt and
braids and chest and knees onto the floor.
They let her go. Diane puts back the jug
and walks away. Small fingerless hands
of smoke grab Diane when she turns
her back and slam her against the white
refrigerator door. They are wrapping
her eyes, throat, arms, stomach, ankles,
hands. They make her open the door and
drink milk, sloppily, milk spilling, drink
milk, drink milk, drink milk, until she's
drenched in sweat, the jug is empty, and
she throws up near the sink, and even
then small fingerless hands of smoke
grab Diane, wrapping her eyes, throat,
arms, stomach, ankles, hands, and slam
her back against the hard refrigerator
door, make her open it, make her drink,
drink it, drink from the empty jug, and
the emptiness spills everywhere as the
lights hum and Diane falls to the floor,
smells that something's been burning all
this time, behind the refrigerator, piles of
dead ants . . .

Small fingerless hands of smoke grab Diane when she stands up and slam her back down against the floor. They are wrapping her eyes, throat, arms, stomach, ankles, hands. She tries to scream for help. They cover her whole body and she feels herself moving somewhere, like milk, she feels like milk moving, and they let her go and she's in a room she's never been in before, a bedroom. She's wearing different clothes, the smoke hands are gone, she gets up and looks out the window. She's looking at her own house. "Fire," she thinks, and nothing happens. Then, she sees herself in the square kitchen window, in the blue refrigerator light, just herself, no hands of smoke, as the door opens and closes, just Diane writhing and drinking the milk, over and over, like possessed.

Blood Diary (Grandmother):

Diane held a magnifying glass, I followed
her behind the fridge, and we looked at the
ants. "Not enough light!" she declared. I
followed her outside and there were more
ants. As we looked at them, they caught
fire under the magnifying glass. Diane
slammed it against the ground, until it
shattered.

BLOOD

The door opens all by itself.

Diane on her bed, knees hiding her face

on the lower bunk.

The top bunk empty.

Diane hears a voice in her mind: "Die."

BLOOD

February 15, 2000

All morning Diane goes around with the smell of stove gas under her nose. No one else can smell it, she thinks. They're all acting normal. But she's acting normal.

Then Diane showers, under the spider in the shower.

BLOOD

July 3, 1996

The bee on the back of Diane's left hand. Wings whirring, the bee lifts up slowly.

Sting and stinger separated by a heart string.

Diane bleeding.

The bee is gone.

Hard mud lit by dew ring of sun. The shape on the back of Diane's hand.

Red flame. Damp tree.

Ever drying, all blood runs.

It hurts.

Blood Diary (Girl Across the Street):

March 8, 1998

Watching from my window as Diane
runs her fingertip back and forth in the
crevice under her right eye . . . I run my
fingertip back and forth in the crevice
under my right eye . . . I want to scream
as loud as I love you.

She takes three steps forward across her
parched yard and looks up. At me. I fall
off the pile of books, hit my head on the
floor.

Blood Diary (Diane):

Diane chewed licorice in the dark, leaning against her empty old crib like a silent movie villain, the flies-in-amber mobile going, chiming a lullaby, and she hummed along too, unraveling the bitter black braids, making faces in the dark that no one could see. It was so bitter . . .

When I walked in and turned on the lights I wasn't there. No licorice, just the old mobile, still moving, above the empty crib. Rain on the window. I took a picture of the room. I am no six-winged girl trapped in a block of amber trapped in a six-year-old's throat. But I miss the taste of licorice in the dark.

I miss my selves, first selves—we believed we'd be me forever. I always dropped the selves close to me for new selves and those for new selves, those for newer selves. A raindrop streaks down the rainy window, picking up other drops, then leaving them behind, as it falls toward the center of the Earth . . .

BLOOD

October 9, 1997

Diane had had two translucent tadpoles.
Head-sized plastic tank on kitchen table.
She could see their silvery hearts beating.
They grew into two opaquer frogs. Big!
Legs, legs! (From tails that self-devour.)

Looking at them, Diane imagined the
ghost of her own tail trailing behind her,
her seconds-ago self on a leash, dragged
inextricably forward. Behind her, the
door opened. Diane turned and looked,
the doorway empty.

One day the one frog ate the other. Well,
Diane came home to see just one where
there'd been two—had there really been
two?

Diane grabbed the frog, fingers ripping
through custom-chemicalled moss, and
held it up in the air (dripping, kicking
slowly), pinched between fingers, under
the rotating ceiling-fan light. Diane
could see the frog's heart pumping blood
through its faintly clear body, but not the
second frog inside.

Diane shuddered and sighed as if she was
in a movie, blown up on a big screen, in
a dark theater, watched by hundreds of
people without faces.

Blood Diary (Diane):

My grandmother took swimming lessons
after a lifetime being afraid of the water.

I was five, and I was six, and I was seven,
I was eight.

My grandmother gave us her broken
piano.

Just like I had different ages, the piano had
different keys.

Loud men and a truck delivered it.

I was drawing eyes on my left hand. I was
pretending it was my sister. When I was
done drawing the eyes it was just a hand,
again, to me.

BLOOD

May 31, 1995

Diane sucks the blood on her finger
after pulling the cuticle off.

Diane's mother stands at the kitchen window,
as the shadow of an airplane
passes over her face.

*

Diane chews a clove of garlic slowly.
Her mouth stings
even after she swallows.

She was the smallest person
at the wedding
and everyone wore white.

*

Diane sits on the top bunk
        and rips a twenty dollar bill in half.

BLOOD

May 30, 1995

Diane remembers the green ball
that went over the neighbor's fence.

She finds a photo of herself
under her mother's pillow.
In it, she's a blur,

> hands up and open in front of her face,
> the background crisp,
> the bottom of a red slide.

> *

From the small light of Diane's window
Diane sees her shadow against the wall.
The shadow opens its mouth—
Diane turns away.

> *

Hot water running cold:
Diane's hands under the tap.

BLOOD

January 1, 1999

Diane breathes on the mirror in her grandmother's old bathroom.
Diane touches one finger to the glass.

She draws a spiral
eye.

Part 4: *Reflection of the half-moon*

BLOOD

Diane's adopted sister lasted
    three days
    before Diane ate her—
boiled potato
    with leeks taped as arms,
    legs, eyebrows,
    hands, feet,
    fingers, toes (smaller and smaller leeks).
    Crunch, crunch, crunch, crunch.
The smelly sister under the bed.
The potato Diane kept
    for weeks under the red shirt she
    tucked into the elastic waistband
    of her night pants.

And Diane whispered,
"Radio silence . . ."

Blood Diary (Girl Across the Street):

November 27, 1998 – 4:16 am

Diane takes off her pajamas and jumps in the pool. A boy jumps in with her. They dance together humming different tunes, Diane holding onto the boy's arms. Gradually Diane hums the boy's songs. Gradually Diane's muscles give out and she can't move anymore. The boy pulls her along, kissing her head, then her neck, then her shoulders, pushing her fingers into his mouth as he sucks them noisily. Diane's head is swiveling manically. The boy convulses. Then the boy disappears under the water, as if pulled. Dark water fills his space. Just Diane standing in the naked pool, alone. And Diane gets out and puts on the boy's clothes and walks back into her house, humming her own song . . .

November 27, 1998 – 4:41 am

From now on I'll have everyone call me Diane.

Blood Diary (Mother):

October 8, 1995

Diane whistles through muddy hands. "Diane, did you ever dream of the bird of the rain?" I ask. "No, Mama," she says, flapping her fingers.

While she's at school, I break open her diary with a knife. She did dream about the bird of the rain! Bitch!

Why did the dream skip over me? My own mother went into the mud as if she was naked, as if I wasn't watching. My mother whistled through her muddy hands and said:

"The bird of the rain is so dark, it's like a hole in the sky. Wherever it flies, it shows the nothing on the other side."

Diane wrote in her diary:
The bird of the rain wants everyone to love each other.
The bird of the rain flew in front of Mama's face,
and I took a picture of it.

I want to stop reading, but I can't. Diane's handwriting is terrible. She filled in all the letter's eyes, black . . .

I rip out the pages. Falling asleep in Diane's bed. Waking up in the dark. Screaming for ten seconds at the storm door.

Diane's back. Dinner. "Why did you lie to me, Diane?" "I thought you would be sad if I dreamed about it and you didn't," she says, mouth full of corn. I slap her.

I wonder if Mama can see anything through the bird
of the rain. It is always right in front of her eyes,
covering everything.

BLOOD

March 17, 1996

Diane remembers the little government offices
in her grandmother's town
ribboned red and green.

Diane doesn't remember
when she learned the color of veins.

After her grandmother's heart attack,
Diane swims in a pool
and finally puts her head under water.

Blood Diary (Diane):

March 16, 1995

My grandmother is going deaf, sitting on
her grandfather's lap on the rocking chair
on the porch looking up at the storm.

She counts out loud after one lightning
strike, waiting for thunder, waiting for
thunder. Ninety-seven, ninety-eight,
ninety-nine, while more lightning
keeps pouring down. She thinks: It must
beinfinitely far, infinitely close.

Her grandfather names the stars through
the clouds: Diane, Diane, Diane, Diane,
Diane, Diane, Die . . .

BLOOD

February 27, 1997

Diane held the snow globe in her hands and shook it. It kept snowing outside even after the snow globe settled . . . Diane adopted a tiny frog and put it in her slipper with grass and some raspberries . . . Diane enjoyed dissecting tadpoles in school . . . Diane showered with her mother's blue swimsuit on. It was too big for her; her shoulders kept falling through . . . Diane dug in the backyard to see how deep she could dig. She wanted to make a hole big enough to stand in. She found an ant colony and they all poured out, up her arms . . . Diane watched the sun set over the water from her attic window . . . Diane listened to her mother's opera records when no one was home . . . Diane spun in circles until she got dizzy, then kept spinning until she blacked out.

Diane stuck her fingers in her ears to see how deep they were.

Blood Diary (Girl Across the Street):

November 27, 1998 – 4:16 am

Diane, are you inside a body—or what's around it?

Diane takes off her motorcycle helmet and jumps in the pool of black jello. A giant praying mantis jumps in with her. They dance together humming different tunes, Diane holding onto the mantis's knife-edge arms. Gradually Diane hums the mantis's songs. Gradually Diane's muscles give out and she can't move anymore. The mantis pulls her along, eating her head, then her neck, then her shoulders, pushing each arm down its gullet as it chomps, head swiveling manically. And when it's eaten her completely, black jello fills the space where she had been, and the mantis gets out and puts on her motorcycle helmet and stands the motorcycle up on its side at the edge of the pool and rides away, humming Diane's song . . .

November 27, 1998 – 4:18 am

From now on I'll have everyone call me Diane.

Blood Diary (Girl Across the Street):

February 12, 1999

I am wearing the black wig I made from old shoelaces colored black.

How wonderful I am.

I am Diane.

I am Diane!

I love feeling how the world turns underneath me.

I love knowing that outside there is an even greater outside.

Outside that there is an inside.

It's my door.

It leads back into my room.

I can come and go whenever I choose, but I don't.

My body is filling up with pink water.

So is the room outside my body, but the water is red, and full of singing anemones.

BLOOD

January 14, 1999

Diane floats up through the clouds and
breaks the surface of the water above her,
on which a moment before she'd seen her
body's silver-winged reflection.

Diane swims to the edge of the pond and
walks out through the sharp gooseberry
bushes, brushing the ticks off, through
the sliding glass doors, up the stairs to
her room. She takes the knife out from
under the pillow. She sits on her bed,
back against the wall, feet hanging over
the edge, dripping. Waiting until the
shadows lengthen and then disappear into
all-dark. (Continual sound of dripping.
The splash of each against floor.)

Diane returns to the middle of the pond,
up to her waist. Scratches all over her
body bleeding. With the knife. Holding
the knife in both hands, pointing down.
The reflection of the half-moon.

BLOOD

March 14, 2006

I.

Diane closes her eyes and sees four round
soap bubbles around an eye-shaped fish.
Horizontal jail bars in the distance move
closer, move through the soap bubbles.
Now it is just Diane and the fish.

II.

Diane sees duck tracks in mud, puts her
finger in the wet mud in one and tastes it.
It is sour. Diane lies down on the tracks,
erasing them with her body. The water
laps her side.

III.

Diane is bending the jail bars with her
hands into the shape of an eye. She walks
through the eye into a room and falls
into its pool of water. The water is bright
blue-green—because of the tiles and
underwater lighting. Looking up from
underwater, she sees four glowing golden
spheres above the water, their images
broken repeatedly-differently by the
ripples. They are not moving. She tries
to swim toward the surface, but the more
she swims the farther the spheres move.
The surface always stays the same distance
from Diane. She finds she is having no
trouble holding her breath.

IV.

Diane stretches her right arm up and cranes her head, chin to collarbone, to look at her armpit. Instead of hair, she sees gray feathers. No, they are white, but it is too dark to see that. She tries to find greater and greater light to look at her armpit. No matter how much sun or how many lights she points, the feathers always look gray.

V.

Diane opens her eyes and walks forward. Her children are waving at her from across the street. There is no crosswalk or light. She stops at the edge of the street and waits for the cars to stop passing so she can run across. The vehicles keep coming. She stops at the edge of the street and waits for the cars to stop passing so she can run across. The vehicles keep coming.

Part 5: *A house inside a house inside Diane*

Blood Diary (Father):

Drooling on a pile of dirty blankets in a
dim blue room, you're awake. *Lion King*
paused on the far wall.

You stagger into the narrow hall, see
yourself in the next room asleep with
our daughter, who at first looks like me,
tangled in blankets too small.

I'm in the living room on a cushionless
futon frame, also watching *The Lion King*.
"Why didn't you come to bed tonight?"
you say. An image: me slipping off a
barrel in the kitchen. I say, "Don't you
remember . . . I think I died." You say,
"How can you know that?" "I have a
vision of it in my head." You see a circle
inside my head with a picture of me in it.

I say, "Do you realize you're dreaming?"
And our daughter knows it's a dream
and is busy trying to construct her own
dream in the corner, saying out loud what
she wants in it. I say, "At first I thought
you died and that was why things kept
repeating with you in them."

And the movie starts over, walking
through its first two scenes, stopping
when it shows you curled tight as a shiver
on the dusty mattress with our daughter.

BLOOD

December 24, 1998

Diane dreamed her mother died. Diane lucid dreamed she adopted a black Labrador. She decided to call it Shithead. Months passed. The dog came running happily whenever she called out over the green hills, "Shit-head!" Spinning around the corner of the shed she kicked Shithead hard, she was so happy. She woke up. She didn't know she was that kind of cruel person. She looked in the public library for movies about people torturing and killing dogs, but all she could find were movies about people who loved dogs. Finally she asked the librarian. The librarian laughed, covered her heart with her hand over name tag ("Diane")—and walked away, shaking her head, wiping a tear from her left eye.

A murder of crows was on the bare tree, outside the library, after dusk. The door Diane let go of slammed. As the crows flew off, Diane saw purple veins of electricity flash and disappear between the branches.

Blood Diary (Mother):

May 27, 2007

Seeing your blurry picture—

the rabbit standing on its shadow
in the garden,
at the end of the garden,
its shadow like ice over water,

and two birds
standing on the highest prickles
of two trees
taking turns talking,
taking turns listening
to the shared air
to the depth of a silence
they never let each other hear,

the trees rising out of the silence
like trees.

Blood Diary (Diane):

March 14, 2005

    I.
In the dark kitchen, scrubbing charred meat off the cast iron.
Time falls
like a rain on the water.

I taste my blackened thumb: ripples.

    II.
A net made of chains;
each chain made of links;
each link with an inner emptiness mirroring the outer: an eye!

Linked together,
they bind us
in love.

    III.
In my dreams I'm throwing around a fist-sized ball so black it
can't be seen
except as the absence of that which it covers,
flying through the air,
from one hand to another—

and in these dreams, always,
I have so many bodies . . .

BLOOD

Undated

Diane turns a hand-crank projector on the stoop of a falling-in cabin surrounded by woods. The long rows of shadows under the many different shapes of trees in the moonlight. She is still conjoined to her other self, who is holding her sister's hand. Who holds the screen down, beige sheet, rippling in the wind, against the trunk of a huge, vermilion oak tree. The film: Diane's birth.

Blood Diary (Diane):

I am standing on the roof of my father's silver car impermanently denting it— holding a dozen orange mesh bags of oranges: in my elbows, hands, under armpits. He's standing in the open doorway of the house and he's also inside the car, craning his neck up to watch from the driver's seat. The Papa watching from the house is six years old. I am six years old but my body is adult, with hair. These are so heavy. I shift on my feet and without meaning to drop a bag and another bag and another until they're all on the ground, oranges rolling down the driveway. I'm my own mother picking them up at the bottom and I'm also still standing on the hot silver car in my bare feet. It's winter but it's 90 degrees, my feet are starting to cook. It smells like carrot cake. It's my birthday. But I'm not born yet. I get off the car and climb into the car. Papa drives me to the hospital. I have scarlet fever. Semi-conscious for twelve days and nights as water slowly fills up the room. When I can't breathe anymore I am making so much sound I realize that I can't hear anything else. Just my fingertips are above the water. The water is unbearably cold.

Blood Diary (Father):

Diane was in the sandbox. It had just rained. She was in her bathing suit. It was 60 degrees and cloudy. There were midges in the sand. She was looking for something with her dark eyes to the sky, looking with her hands. Tongue out in concentration. I looked deeper, leaning so far over the sandbox I had to use my cane to steady myself. I saw a puddle of water forming and deepening where my Diane was digging. "This is our home," she said, as midges drank from its edges.

BLOOD

April 9, 1997

Diane stood in her mother's shadow in the park—matching black skirts and clogs. The sun went behind clouds. It started to snow. The first snowflakes melted when they touched the dandelions. When the snow started to stick, whiting the green field, Diane looked at her hand in her mother's hand. Turning red—the snowflakes dissolved into their skin, like blood.

Diane's mother pulled Diane's hood up, pulled her into an empty pavilion in the middle of the field. Inside, Diane, teeth chattering, saw the pavilion was full of people, their teeth chattering. No—these were skeletons, no skin, no muscle, no organs or nerves. A clacking of bones as they clutched at each other for warmth.

"I can save you!" Diane said, pulling her hand out of her mother's. And Diane dragged the nearest skeleton, by the wrist, outside, holding it up under the snow.

As snowflakes fell and dissolved, red, on the skeleton—skin grew, muscle grew, then nerves. The nerves were on the outside, and kept growing thicker, a root-like tangle. This body screamed, screamed, and attacked Diane, so Diane pulled it apart and it collapsed in a pile of bones and organs on the snow.

Diane limped back into the pavilion. Her mother nowhere to be seen. Diane saw a skeleton clutching a robin inside its chest. "I don't know if you're my mama," Diane said, "but I can't help you. I'm sorry. I would just hurt you. I'm sorry."

The skeleton ran out, past Diane, through the snow. Diane ran after it and put her hands over her eyes, running all the way to the edge of the field. She was so cold by the time she took her hands off her eyes she saw the snow wasn't melting on her anymore, but sticking, white. On her clothes, on her knees, legs, and arms. Diane's mother stood next to Diane, but Diane couldn't see her, both completely covered in snow.

They walked home and there the snow melted and the bathroom rug was stained red. These two women, one half the other's height, standing in front of the filling bathtub, waiting for it to fill.

Blood Diary (Diane):

I tear my grandparents' door from its hinges and throw it into the pond. I kick out from the stone steps in their once yard, swim and grab the door.

I'm knocking on their door again, on my stomach on it, and kicking us towards the island, of wild blackberries. All the houses around the shore are abandoned. I'm hoping the door will open, into the past. I know the door won't open but I'm knocking anyway.

When I get to blackberry island, the water's pulled most of the shore away. By now it's just five feet across, covered with goose shit, with three trees. The other trees are rotting standing upright in the water in rings around blackberry island. Eels, dark green eels gather near the shallow sands there, swim through their roots.

I've stepped on a blackberry. I pick a few blackberries off the ground. They're so soft the petals of their skins fall off their globules like a black rain. Anyway, I put the bunch of them in my mouth and suck out the juice, they collapse, then I chew what's left—as the door floats away, until I can no longer see it, covered by waves.

BLOOD

Diane stood on the beach during an earthquake and felt the dunes shifting beneath her. She slid all the way from the top of the hill to the shoreline, where all of us stood in a huge crowd. The water was pulling back, pulling back, receding, disappearing, draining into a hole in the bottom of the sea. Then, Diane looked on the horizon and saw the sunset obscured, there was a big, big wave coming, and the red sun was shining through it like blood, like a beating heart. Diane woke up, sweating, feeling like it was her own heart beating so fast and tight in that far, rising wave.

Blood Diary (Girl Across the Street):

March 28, 2001

Diane was still breathing
out red mist
as she hung
larger than life

over my house

and the moon went up
shining through her

lighting up her red sprays of breath

when nothing else would be seen

except the utter black
of my fingers spread across the windowpane.

Blood Diary (Girl Across the Street):

December 9, 2001

A house inside a house inside Diane, who runs toward me like a rooster, wobbling.

Somehow she gets into our house, though she's supposed to be long-dead . . .

I locked all the inner doors and my family huddles behind the island in the kitchen.

Diane still finds us, opening her bloody mouth.

Blood Diary (Diane):

March 14, 1993

Blood moon coming, half-moon.

I am like the half-moon.

I am coming to
kill what I love.

Diane's Playlist

A list of songs Diane obsessively compiled during the stage of her disappearance at which she realized that she had disappeared. She knew she could never come back, at least not to the way she was, but the songs made her feel real.

1. "Blue Skies," Willie Nelson
2. "No the End Is Not Near," Benny Hester
3. "On the Beach," Neil Young
4. "Spiral of Ants," Lemon Demon
5. "Pedal Baskets," Brittle Brian
6. "Ambulance," TV on the Radio
7. "I'd Like to Walk Around in Your Mind," Vashti Bunyan
8. "waking up in the park," j'san
9. "Strange," Patsy Cline
10. "La Mer," Nine Inch Nails
11. "Running from Home," Bert Jansch
12. "Oh Baby," Micachu & the Shapes
13. "If We Hold on Together," Diana Ross
14. "I'm Looking Out for Me," Gilbert Gottfried
15. "Blister in the Sun," Violent Femmes
16. "blisters," serpentwithfeet
17. "Just the Two of Us," Grover Washington Jr.
18. "Girls," Death in Vegas
19. "Bop Bop," Mean Lady
20. "God Only Knows," Claudine Longet
21. "Wes Anderson," Misc.
22. "Black Hole Sun," Scott Bradlee's Postmodern Jukebox
23. "Will You Still Love Me Tomorrow," Roberta Flack
24. "I Can Feel the Ice Melting," Yo La Tengo
25. "Kuhstall-Jodler," Grenzland Sextett aus Tirol
26. "Dream Care," Cloud Central
27. "I Hope I Think of Bike Riding When I'm Dying," Neat Beats
28. "Conceptual Romance," Jenny Hval
29. "Winter," The Dodos

30. "Bohemian Dances," The Do
31. "Waveland," Noam Pikelny
32. "Soft Stuff," Emily Yacina
33. "Waters of March," Art Garfunkel
34. "A Silver Song," Conspiracy of Owls
35. "Is That All There Is," Peggy Lee
36. "Wanderer Wandering," Slow Club